To My Daughter:

_____

With Love From:

_____

Date:

_____

DAUGHTER

A Keepsake Book

Written by Marie D. Jones

www.debbiemumm.com

new seasons®

ISBN-13: 978-1-4127-9008-6
ISBN-10:1-4127-9008-5

❀ Contents ❀

Meeting You, Meeting Me.........................8

Growing With You 22

Caring and Sharing 34

Days to Celebrate 46

Forever Friends 64

Special Notes 76

Meeting You, Meeting Me

Place Photo Here

First Steps

When I found out you were a girl, I _____

_____

_____

_____

The first time I saw you, I felt _____

_____

_____

_____

_____

Why we chose your name _____

_____

_____

_____

_____

Nicknames and sweet endearments _____

_____

_____

_____

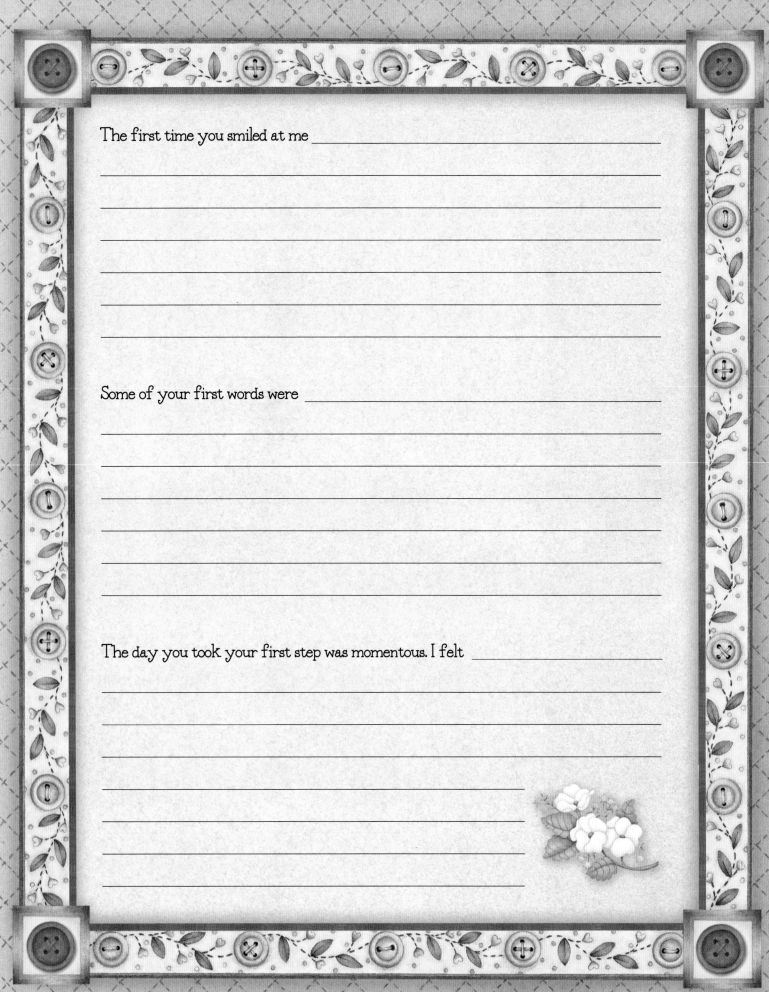

The first time you smiled at me _____

_____

_____

_____

_____

_____

_____

Some of your first words were _____

_____

_____

_____

_____

_____

_____

The day you took your first step was momentous. I felt _____

_____

_____

_____

_____

_____

_____

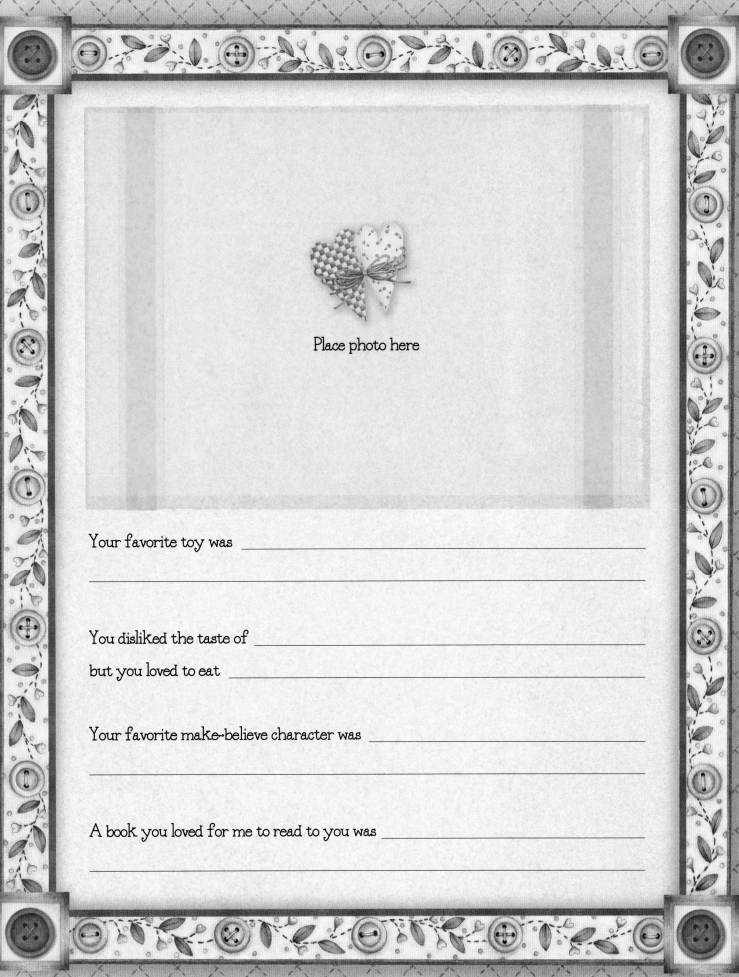

Place photo here

Your favorite toy was _____

_____

You disliked the taste of _____

but you loved to eat _____

Your favorite make-believe character was _____

_____

A book you loved for me to read to you was _____

_____

I could always comfort you by _____

_____

_____

_____

_____

_____

I loved to sing you this lullaby _____

_____

_____

_____

_____

Our quiet moments together were precious to me. I often thought _____

_____

_____

_____

_____

_____

_____

_____

_____

 # Sweet Little Girl

What it means to me to have a daughter _____

_____

_____

_____

_____

My hopes and dreams for you, my little girl_____

_____

_____

_____

_____

_____

_____

_____

_____

_____

_____

_____

The Magic Moment

A rainbow, a shining full moon, or a fresh snowfall is a new discovery for a child. I remember when you first discovered _____

_____

_____

_____

_____

_____

Your favorite Halloween costume was _____

_____

_____

_____

_____

_____

The look in your eyes on holidays when you opened presents_____

_____

_____

_____

_____

When you began to socialize with other children a whole new world opened up for you.
I remember your playmates_____

_____

_____

_____

_____

The playground always filled you with excitement. You loved to play on the_____

_____

_____

_____

The day you got a pet was special because _____

_____

_____

_____

_____

Off to School!

Place Photo Here

On your first day of school you were _____

_____

_____

_____

_____

Your first school friend was _____

_____

A field trip that you couldn't stop talking about was _____

_____

_____

_____

Your favorite teacher was _____

_____

_____

_____

I was glad you were in that class because _____

_____

_____

I was delighted when you brought home this handmade treasure from school _____

_____

_____

_____

A class project we did together _____

_____

_____

_____

_____

A school award you were proud of _____

_____

_____

_____

This is the type of student you were_____

_____

_____

_____

Here is a description of how you dressed for school_____

_____

_____

_____

_____

You started to get homework in this grade_____

_____

_____

_____

_____

_____

Your favorite games at recess were _____

_____

_____

_____

This is what I packed for your lunch _____

_____

_____

_____

_____

Beyond classroom studies, these were the school activities that you enjoyed most

_____

_____

_____

_____

_____

_____

_____

_____

_____

_____

❀ Exploring Life Together ❀

You loved reading and learning about _____

_____

_____

_____

The hardest question you ever asked me was _____

_____

_____

_____

You were always fascinated by _____

_____

_____

_____

_____

As a child you were afraid of _____

but you were brave when you_____

_____

_____

_____

You could spend hours busy with a childhood hobby. You especially liked to_____

_____

_____

_____

One of your favorite games was _____

_____

_____

A special meal or treat we enjoyed cooking together was _____

_____

_____

_____

Trips to the zoo were amazing experiences for you. Your favorite animals were_____

_____

_____

_____

_____

You loved to collect _____

_____

_____

_____

Growing With You

Place Photo Here

Two of a Kind

I knew you took after me the time you _____

_____

_____

_____

_____

_____

I most see myself in you when _____

_____

_____

_____

_____

_____

The trait I am glad you inherited from me is _____

_____

_____

_____

_____

_____

Ways we are alike _____

_____

_____

_____

_____

_____

What's different about you that I admire_____

_____

_____

_____

_____

_____

Each of us has special qualities that make us unique. You just wouldn't be you if

you didn't _____

_____

_____

_____

_____

_____

_____

We share the same ability to _____

_____

_____

_____

_____

Some of your favorite things _____

_____

_____

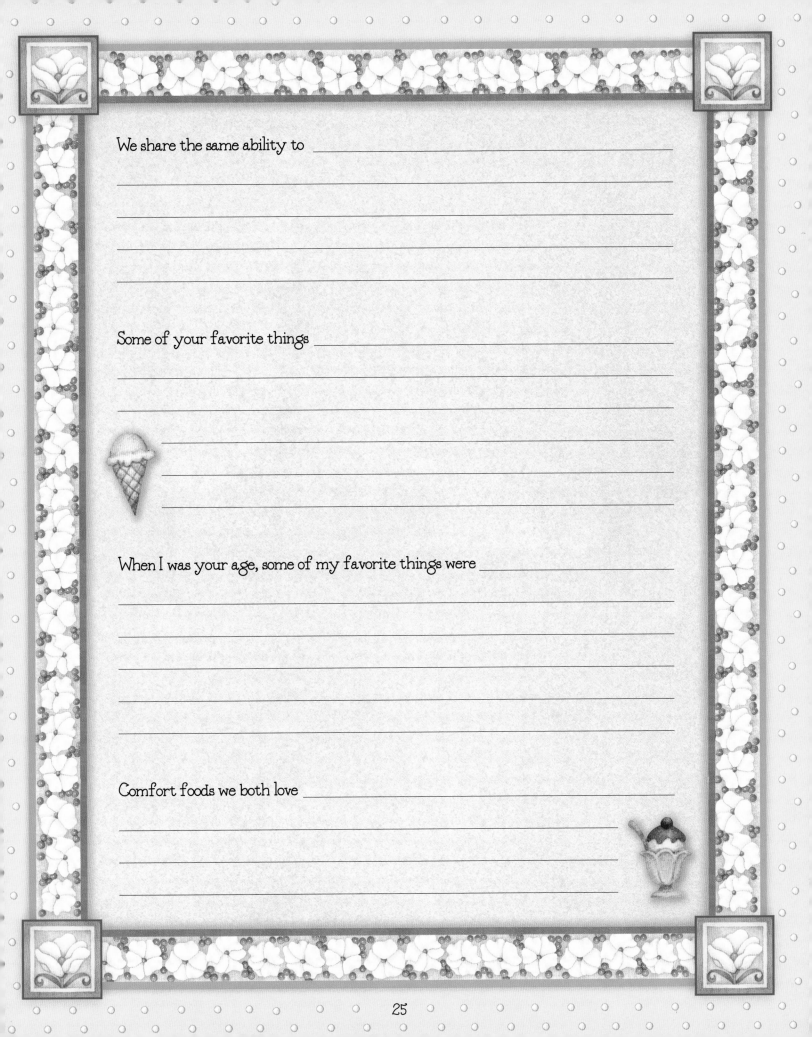

_____

_____

_____

When I was your age, some of my favorite things were _____

_____

_____

_____

_____

_____

Comfort foods we both love _____

_____

_____

_____

Too Proud for Words

Place Photo Here

I knew you were talented when you _____
_____
_____
_____

As you grew, so did your talents. As your talents developed, I felt _____
_____
_____
_____

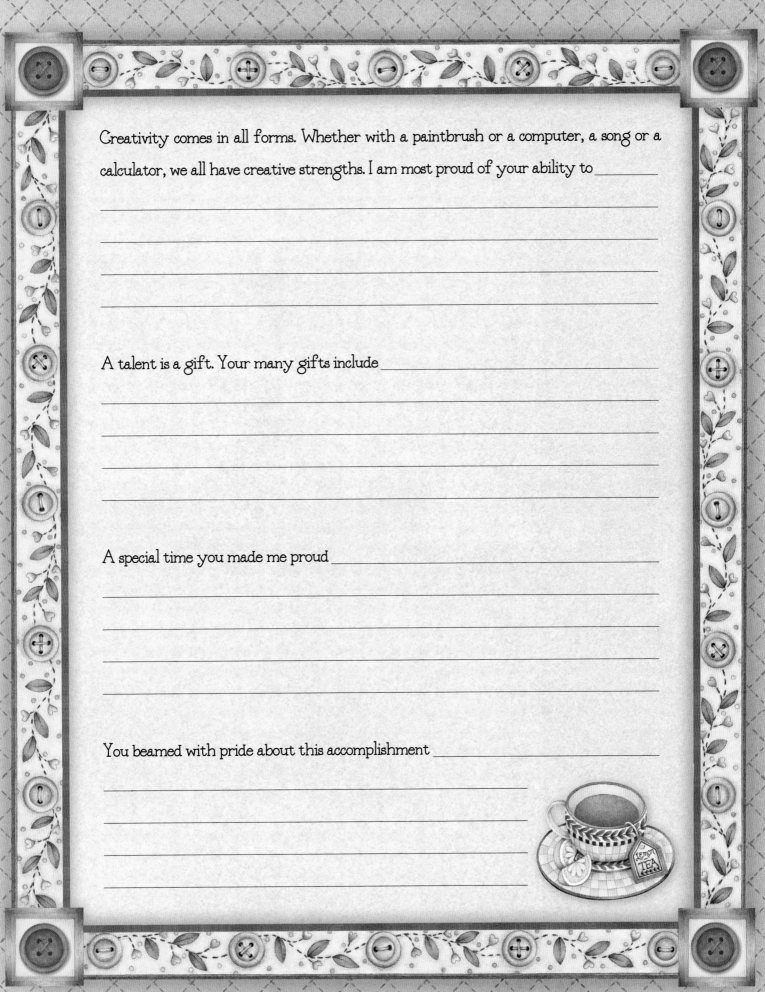

Creativity comes in all forms. Whether with a paintbrush or a computer, a song or a calculator, we all have creative strengths. I am most proud of your ability to _____

_____

_____

_____

_____

A talent is a gift. Your many gifts include _____

_____

_____

_____

_____

A special time you made me proud _____

_____

_____

_____

_____

You beamed with pride about this accomplishment _____

_____

_____

_____

_____

The little things you didn't know I noticed, but meant so much to me _____

_____

_____

_____

_____

I loved to brag about your _____

_____

_____

_____

_____

You were such a show-off when _____

_____

_____

_____

_____

I was privileged to watch you grow from a precocious child into a very special young

woman. I was especially proud just to know you when _____

_____

_____

_____

_____

All Grown Up

I knew you were no longer a child when _____

_____

_____

_____

_____

You seemed wise for your age when you _____

_____

_____

_____

_____

_____

A teen idol you were so crazy about was_____,

while I preferred_____when I was young.

The first time you wore makeup I felt _____

_____

_____

_____

_____

_____

The day you went on your first date_____

_____

_____

_____

_____

_____

_____

Those first teenage crushes are the sweetest and the most heartbreaking.

The first time you got a broken heart _____

_____

_____

_____

_____

I'll never forget when you got your driver's license _____

_____

_____

_____

_____

Your first job was a big step in becoming a grown-up. On the first day of work _____

_____

_____

_____

_____

_____

_____

_____

I suddenly realized you were truly a young woman when _____

_____

_____

_____

_____

_____

_____

_____

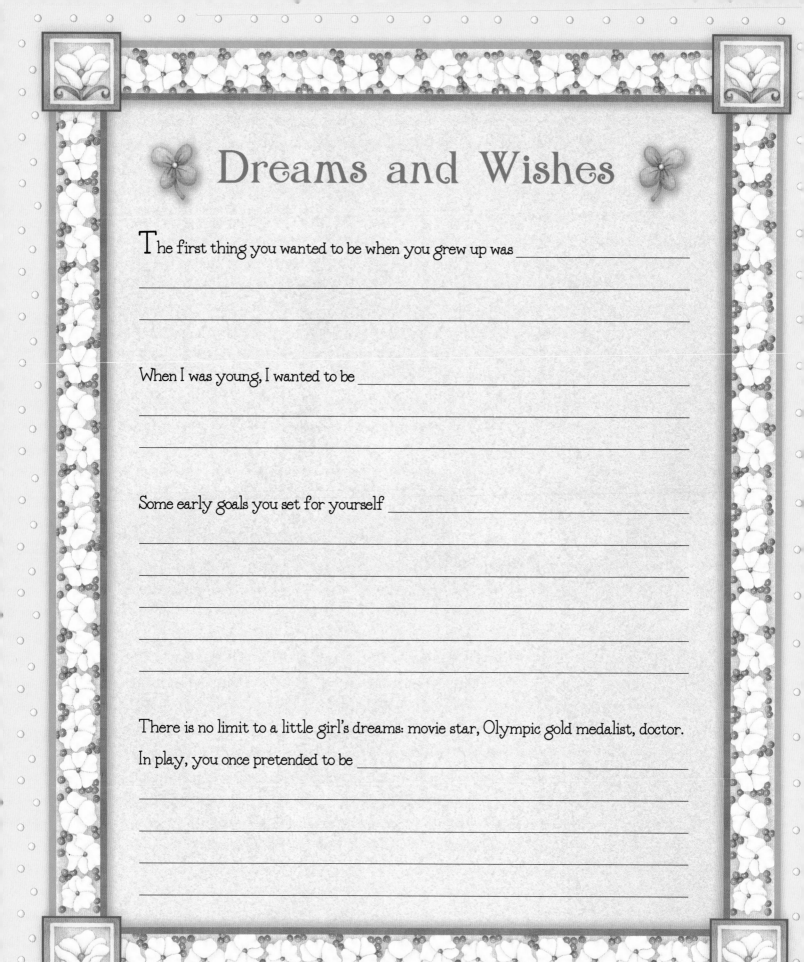

Dreams and Wishes

The first thing you wanted to be when you grew up was _____

_____

_____

When I was young, I wanted to be _____

_____

_____

Some early goals you set for yourself _____

_____

_____

_____

_____

_____

There is no limit to a little girl's dreams: movie star, Olympic gold medalist, doctor.

In play, you once pretended to be _____

_____

_____

_____

_____

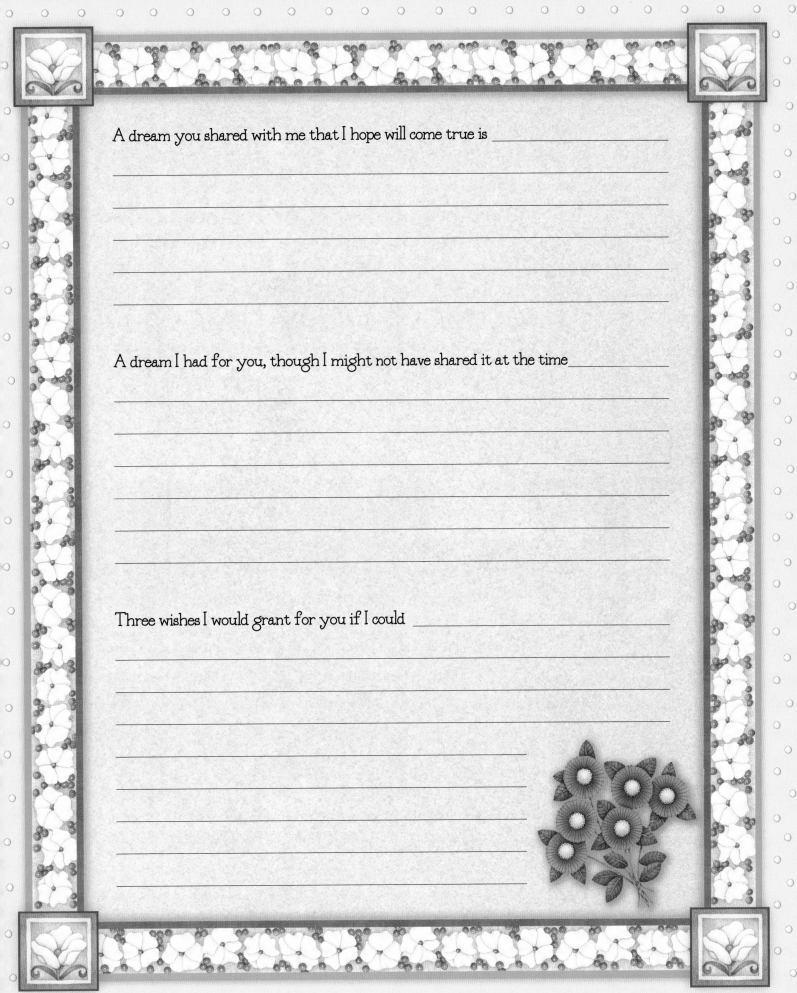

A dream you shared with me that I hope will come true is _____

_____

_____

_____

_____

_____

A dream I had for you, though I might not have shared it at the time_____

_____

_____

_____

_____

_____

Three wishes I would grant for you if I could _____

_____

_____

_____

_____

_____

_____

Caring and Sharing

Place Photo Here

You Can Count on Me

A difficult time you helped me get through _____

_____

_____

_____

_____

I knew I could count on you when _____

_____

_____

_____

_____

A hurdle you faced that you handled with such maturity was _____

_____

_____

_____

You needed me to comfort you when _____

_____

_____

_____

_____

A challenging event we helped each other overcome _____

_____

_____

_____

_____

_____

It felt so good to help you meet your goal when_____

_____

_____

_____

_____

_____

You could always turn a negative into a positive by_____

_____

_____

_____

_____

_____

I can always boost your confidence by _____

_____

_____

_____

_____

_____

_____

When you needed advice on _____

_____

_____,

I was glad you turned to me because _____

_____

_____

_____

_____

_____

_____

It was special when you shared this with me _____

_____

_____

_____

_____

_____

_____

_____

_____

_____

I love how we always support each other when it comes to _____

_____

_____

_____

_____

_____

_____

_____

_____

_____

Learning From Each Other

If I could teach you one thing, it would be _____

_____

_____

_____

_____

_____

It is not always the adult who is the teacher. A lesson you taught me was_____

_____

_____

_____

_____

_____

I never imagined I would learn this new skill from my own daughter_____

_____

_____

_____

_____

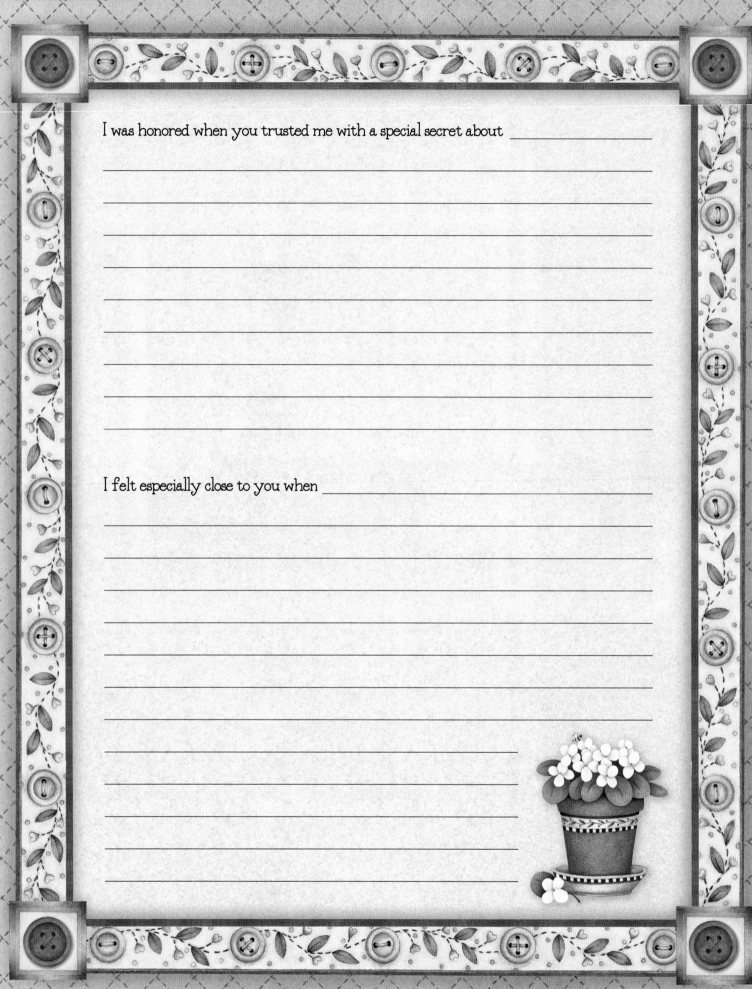

I was honored when you trusted me with a special secret about _____

_____

_____

_____

_____

_____

_____

_____

I felt especially close to you when _____

_____

_____

_____

_____

_____

_____

_____

_____

Our favorite movie to watch together _____

_____

_____

_____

_____

A special way we connect _____

_____

_____

_____

_____

_____

_____

_____

_____

The most meaningful gift you ever gave me was _____

_____

_____

_____

_____

_____

_____

Laughter is the Best Medicine

We ended up laughing about this embarrassing moment _____

_____

_____

_____

_____

You always seemed happiest when _____

_____

_____

_____

We could never resist teasing each other about _____

_____

_____

_____

Even moments of quiet contentment are special, like the time we _____

_____

_____

_____

Can You Believe
We Did That?

Our trip turned into an adventure when _____
_____
_____
_____
_____

A daring thing you did that I could never do_____
_____
_____
_____

We had so much fun when we both refused to act our ages_____
_____
_____
_____

A time you challenged me to do something new _____
_____
_____
_____

Days to Celebrate

Place Photo Here

Where the Day Takes You

Our favorite way to spend a rainy day was _____

_____

_____

_____

_____

Our most memorable weekend activities were _____

_____

_____

_____

_____

_____

_____

_____

A vacation that we never wanted to end was _____

_____

_____

_____

_____

_____

_____

_____

Even short trips or errands gave us time to talk

in the car. I loved our chats about _____

_____

_____

_____

_____

_____

_____

_____

Party Girl

A birthday party I will never forget _____

_____

_____

_____

_____

_____

_____

_____

_____

Fashions change, but dressing up for parties is always fun. Your favorite party dress or outfit was _____

_____

_____

_____

_____

_____

_____

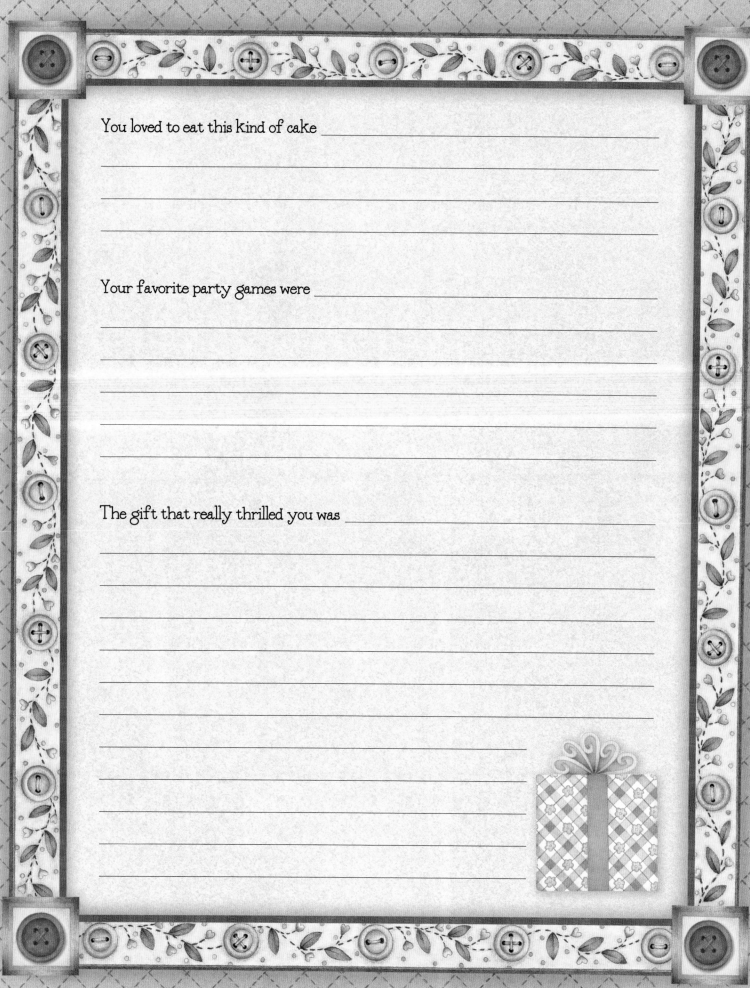

You loved to eat this kind of cake _____

_____

_____

_____

Your favorite party games were _____

_____

_____

_____

_____

_____

The gift that really thrilled you was _____

_____

_____

_____

_____

_____

_____

_____

_____

_____

Slumber parties were fun when you were young. I remember when_____

_____

_____

_____

_____

_____

_____

Eventually you felt "too old" to have a slumber party. When you attended teen parties,

I felt_____

_____

_____

_____

I remember how excited you were about this school dance_____

_____

_____

_____

_____

_____

Out and About

We had a blast dressing up for special events. You used to love to borrow my
_____, and I always
wished I could wear your _____
_____
_____

I'll never forget the night we went to this special event together _____
_____
_____
_____
_____
_____
_____
_____
_____

Our favorite place to eat out together was _____
_____
_____
_____

 # You Did It!

An accomplishment you were most proud of in school was_____

_____

_____

_____

_____

_____

The day you graduated from high school, I was bursting with pride_____

_____

_____

_____

_____

_____

_____

_____

_____

53

Place Photo Here

You were so excited the day you finally _____

_____

_____

_____

_____

I was never more proud of you than when _____

_____

_____

_____

_____

A special achievement you couldn't wait to share _____

_____

_____

_____

_____

_____

The day you moved into a place of your own, I felt _____

_____

_____

_____

_____

_____

_____

Your first car was _____

_____

_____

_____

_____

Reaching Higher

When you got into college, I _____

_____

_____

_____

Here is a description of the campus _____

_____

_____

_____

_____

The day you left for college _____

_____

_____

_____

_____

_____

_____

_____

I was worried about _____

_____

_____

_____

_____

_____

_____

I was excited about_____

_____

_____

_____

_____

_____

_____

_____

_____

_____

_____

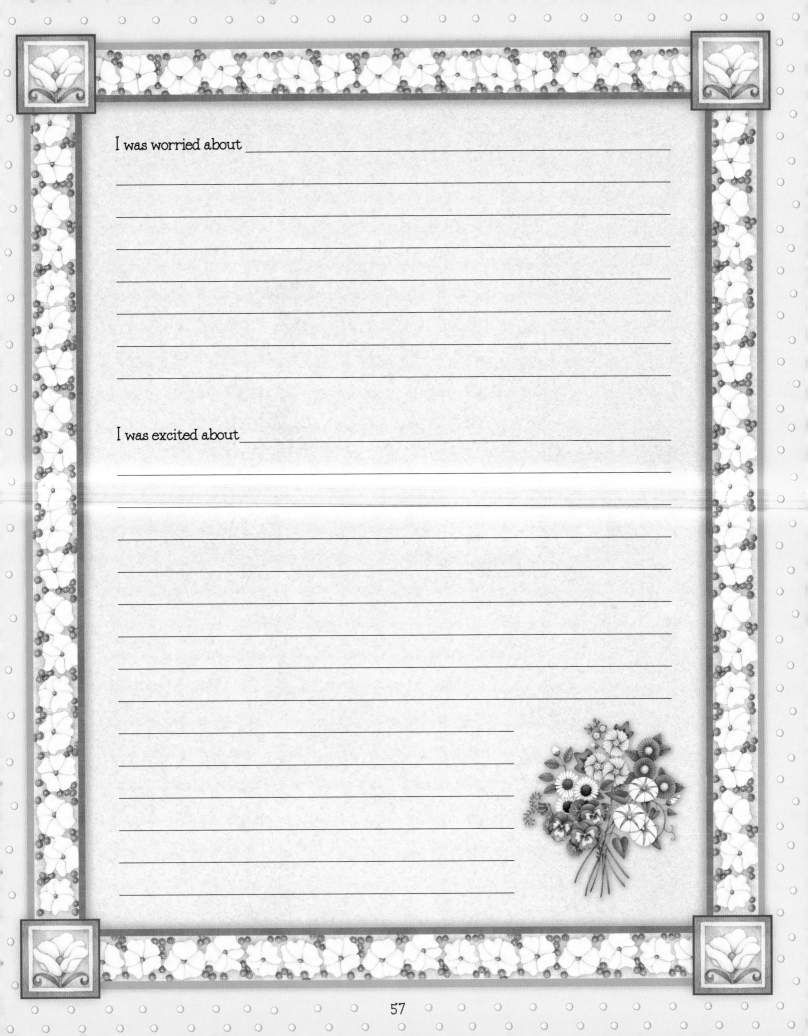

The professor that most influenced your life decisions was _____

_____

_____

_____

_____

_____

I was glad you had this professor because _____

_____

_____

_____

You really enjoyed this aspect of college _____

_____

_____

_____

_____

_____

_____

_____

_____

_____

_____

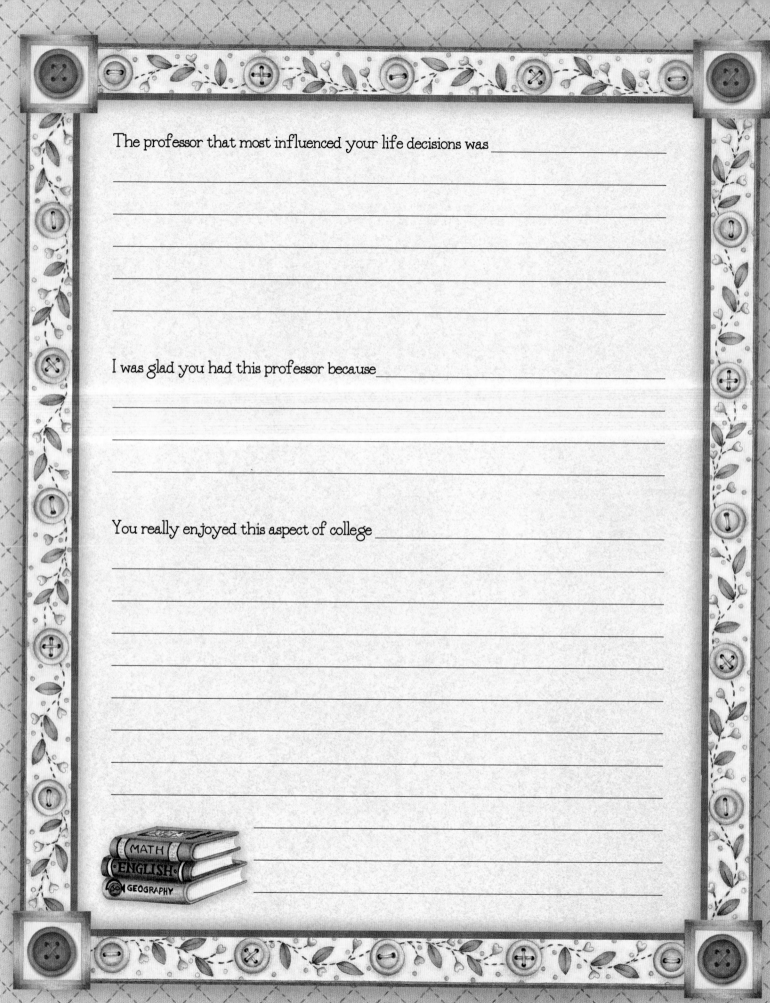

Your first roommate was _____

_____

_____

_____

I was glad you participated in these extracurricular events _____

_____

_____

_____

_____

_____

When I visited you _____

_____

_____

_____

_____

_____

_____

_____

_____

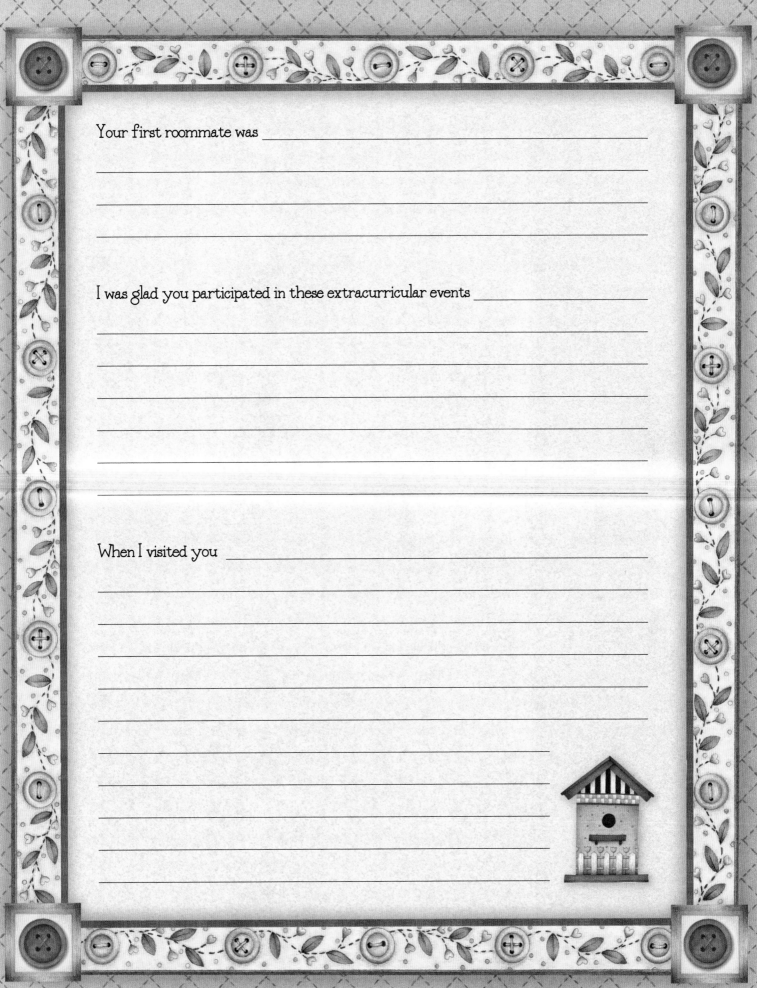

The Corporate Ladder

Your first career-related position was _____

_____

_____

_____

_____

A difficulty you encountered early in your career was _____

_____

_____

_____

_____

_____

_____

You handled this situation by _____

_____

_____

_____

_____

_____

When you got the job you wanted _____

_____

_____

_____

A promotion you were excited about was _____

_____

_____

All of your hard work really paid off when _____

_____

_____

_____

You never gave up your dream to _____

_____

_____

_____

_____

_____

_____

_____

The Big Event

When you told me you were in love, I felt _____

_____

_____

_____

_____

_____

_____

The day you told me you were engaged, I _____

_____

_____

_____

_____

_____

_____

_____

_____

_____

_____

_____

On your wedding day, I felt so many things _____

_____

_____

_____

_____

_____

_____

_____

My words of wisdom for you as you set forth on your journey of marriage _____

_____

_____

_____

_____

_____

_____

_____

_____

Forever Friends

Place Photo Here

Daughter, Woman, Friend

Our mother-daughter relationship has transformed into _____

_____

_____

_____

_____

_____

In some ways I still see you as my little girl, especially when _____

_____

_____

_____

_____

_____

A girlish quality I hope you never lose _____

_____

_____

_____

_____

_____

I knew you had become a good friend when _____

_____

_____

_____

_____

_____

As adults, I love it when we relate by _____

_____

_____

_____

_____

Now that you are grown up, we have even more in common _____

_____

_____

_____

_____

_____

A special hobby we share _____

_____

_____

_____

_____

_____

My favorite way to spend a day with you _____

_____

_____

_____

_____

_____

_____

Something we do each year that I always look forward to_____

_____

_____

_____

_____

_____

_____

_____

Building New Bridges

The day you became a mother, I felt _____
_____
_____
_____
_____

I hope you will teach your child _____
_____
_____
_____
_____

I hope your child will teach you _____
_____
_____
_____
_____
_____
_____

Motherhood has made you different in that you _____

_____

_____

_____

_____

_____

Now that you are a mom, you can understand why I always _____

_____

_____

_____

_____

_____

I wish you a long life, a happy marriage, and successful parenthood. My best advice

to you is _____

_____

_____

_____

_____

_____

What being a grandmother means to me _____

_____

_____

_____

_____

_____

I've always loved the way you relate to your own grandparents _____

_____

_____

_____

_____

_____

_____

I hope that my relationship with your child will be _____

_____

_____

_____

_____

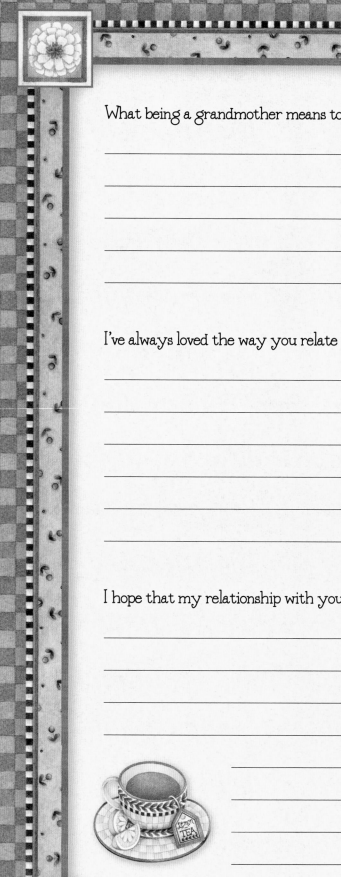

_____

_____

_____

_____

If I Could Tell You

Here are some of the many things that I love about you _____

_____

_____

_____

I have long admired this special quality of yours _____

_____

_____

_____

I am grateful to have you as a daughter because _____

_____

_____

_____

I have always wanted to tell you that _____

_____

_____

_____

_____

_____

In difficult times, I hope you will remember _____

_____

_____

_____

_____

A dream for you that recently came true is _____

_____

_____

_____

_____

_____

If there is one thing to remember about life, it is this _____

_____

_____

_____

_____

_____

_____

_____

This is what I hope I have taught you _____

_____

_____

_____

_____

_____

I am most proud to have taught you this _____

_____

_____

_____

_____

When you think of me, I hope you will remember _____

_____

_____

_____

_____

_____

_____

_____

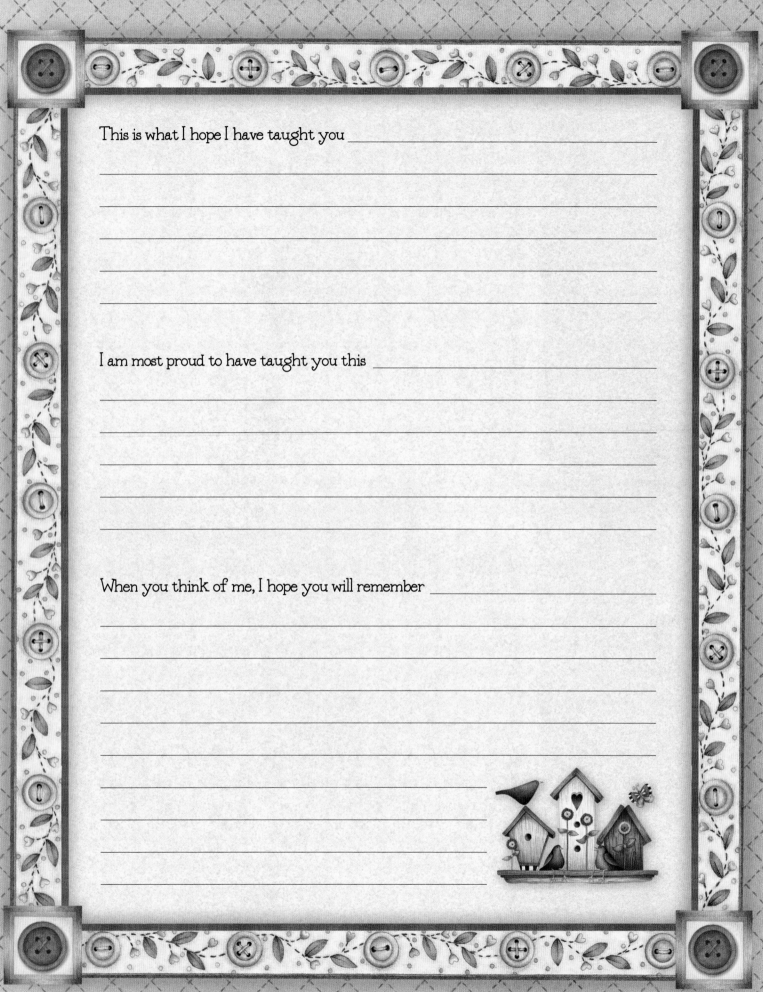

 # SPECIAL NOTES

Here is a place for you to write a special message to your daughter.
Use these pages to say something you've never said or perhaps do not say enough.

· · ·

_____

_____

_____

_____

_____

_____

_____

_____

_____

_____

_____

_____

_____

_____

_____

_____

_____